As well as ten collecti~on or before the~ ~y Cronin has~ written a number of ~already r~ , including biographies of Flann O'Brien and Sa~muel~ Beckett. He is also the author of *Dead as Doornails,* the classic memoir of Dublin's arts scene in the fifties, as well as numerous essays, and a novel, *The Life of Riley.* He is married to the writer Anne Haverty and lives in Dublin. He served as a cultural and artistic advisor to the Irish Government in the 1980s, and was a founding member of Aosdána, where he has been elected as Saoi, a distinction conferred for exceptional artistic achievement. In 1983 he received the Marten Toonder Award for his contribution to Irish literature.

Praise for Anthony Cronin

'Cronin is one of our finest and most dedicated poets, his work stretching back more than fifty years to a time of unequivocal reality. His warm commitment and tenacious artistry remind us of the supreme value of the enterprise.'

– Derek Mahon

'What I value most is the thrill of his use of language, the pitch of one man's unmistakable voice.'

– Paul Durcan

'We need him. Not a poet in Ireland should feel confident he is better.'

– James Simmons

'It is as if some of the strenuum of the best Irish prose had entered the verse at last.'

– C. H. Sisson

'Cronin has produced one of the most distinctive and essential poetic oeuvres of Irish poetry in recent decades.'

– Michael O'Loughlin

'Anthony Cronin has always been brisk, impatient with sentiment, as sure of himself and his vision of truth as the Prophet Isaiah was. He carries a formidable intelligence with a deceptive modesty.'

– Theo Dorgan, *Irish Independent*

'Cronin's long poems in particular [...] stand out as a distinctive achievement. Their lucid arguments, muscular but accessible language, technical skill and wry engagement with the contemporary world [...] occupy their own space with an impressive confidence.'

— Fintan O'Toole, *The Irish Times*

'Anthony Cronin is of the first kind, a thinking man who happens to be a poet and a remarkably fine one at that... *The End of the Modern World* is a tortured meditation on the loss of an ideal that was never fully embodied... Cronin's is a major voice: he is Ireland's modern Dryden, a master of the public word in the public place.'

— George Szirtes, *The Irish Times*

The End of the Modern World

Anthony Cronin

NEW ISLAND

THE END OF THE MODERN WORLD

First published in 2016 by
New Island Books
16 Priory Hall Office Park
Stillorgan
County Dublin
Republic of Ireland

www.newisland.ie

PRINT ISBN: 978 1 84840 524 0
EPUB ISBN: 978 1 84840 525 7
MOBI ISBN: 978 1 84840 526 4

British Library Cataloguing Data.
A CIP catalogue record for this book is available from the British Library.

Typeset by JVR Creative India
Cover design by Shauna Daly
Printed by SPRINT-print Ltd.

10 9 8 7 6 5 4 3 2 1

Preface

Michael O'Loughlin

The End of the Modern World, one of the most exciting achievements in Irish poetry of the last century, makes its first appearance here as a single volume.

Ambitious long poems such as this are a notoriously tricky form in which few twentieth century poets have succeeded. In many cases the failure is due to an over-burdened design collapsing under the pressure of the content. As Ezra Pound mournfully said in his famous long poem, *The Cantos*, 'I cannot make it cohere'.

Having already written one of the major long poems of our times, *R.M.S Titanic*, Anthony Cronin expertly overcomes this pitfall once again. His themes in *The End of the Modern World* are various but compulsively intertwined – the relationship between the sexes, the rise of capitalism, the meaning of the modern – but for form he has chosen the simple, functional, red-brick unit of the unrhymed sonnet, democratic and direct. He calls the whole a sonnet sequence, and as the poem progresses it forms an organic whole. Yet again, triumphantly, Anthony Cronin makes it cohere.

The title of this elegy for modernism implicitly asks the question: where and when did the modern world have its beginning? Cronin locates it and begins his poem in the feudal world, which created the nexus of power and sex called chivalry, and its expression in courtly love, from which much of the structure of western poetry ultimately derives. The history of courtly love is an essential part of the history of capitalism, the place where sex meets market forces and becomes another commodity in developing capitalist culture. He embarks on this epic pilgrimage through our modern world with the lines:

> *The clinging, clayey soils of our wet north*
> *Defeated Roman farmers...*

This implies that by escaping Roman occupation and feudalism, Ireland's history would become marginal to the rise of the modern.

Cronin vividly expresses how sex and power conjoin in the most elementary ways. After a bravura opening the poem proceeds in hypnotically musical and muscular iambics through the succeeding centuries of tangled and knotted relationships between the sexes and class conflict. Many memorable and public figures find their place in this essence of the history of western civilization: Picasso, Lenin, De Sade, Marinetti, Van Gogh, and Elvis ('The Liberated Liberator'). But more than any of them, the guiding spirit throughout the work is Baudelaire, the High Priest of the modern. In one of the many striking vignettes this work is so rich in, we first encounter Baudelaire on the Parisian barricades of 1848, equipped with double-barrelled gun and cartridge belt.

Anthony Cronin has never been fixated on the 'matter of Ireland' and, characteristically, when Ireland does appear on this world stage, it is in the beguiling form of Robert Emmet, that most ambiguous and enigmatic of Irish heroes, claiming that:

> *Your other sad rebellions had been raised*
> *For rural reasons. Mine at least were modern.*
> *My mob was European, avant-garde.*

By the time this astonishing journey arrives at the late twentieth century, the poet himself appears, returning to live in Ireland in the 1970s. By now, the poet's perspective is no longer Yeats pacing the battlements of his tower, but Cronin facing the wall of the back bedroom of 51 Stella Gardens in Irishtown. In those decades of the 70s and 80s, the poem wrestles with the thorny problem of the public and the private and the poet's role in all of this. A familiar ghost reproaches him:

> *'That's phony, all that politics and stuff.'*
> *It wasn't, but I felt a traitor to*
> *The long tradition of the man alone,*
> *Deriding all sides, driven out by all,*
> *To feast on his own heart in scorn and joy…*

One of the great triumphs of *The End of the Modern World* is how it seamlessly merges the personal and political into such pure poetry. As the sequence continues towards the present, Cronin takes up the old symbol of the Dark Tower to which Childe Roland came, and makes it a symbol of corporate capitalism, a gleaming tower of glass and steel. Roland becomes an eager executive, a latter-day knight. The sequence ends, unsettlingly prescient, with Manhattan and its towers as those shining symbols of late capitalism:

> *Rise in resplendence, such a culmination*
> *Of history, seen at sunset from the harbour*
> *Meaningless, astonishing and simple.*

I

1.

The clinging, clayey soils of our wet north
Defeated Roman farmers and the rain
Which swept in from the west made swamp of fen
Until the mould-board plough dragged through the mud
By wretched rows of oxen tied together,
Raised ridges in the worst of fields, the flattest,
Which drained the water from the land. The low-skied
North then found the rain a virtue. Twice a year,
Both in the quickening showers of spring and later,
In that queer stillness of a fine October
When autumn gutters out behind the trees,
Ploughs could be run. This haunted north, more fertile
Than ever the ghost-free south, gave forth a surplus
Which fed new ghosts, great visions, dreams, desirings.

2.

But first the fields had to expand, the manor
Lord had to make the laws which marked out strips,
Long, narrow, straight, for cultivation by
The teams of beasts which they now yoked and shared.
Loving the bounds that now were set to nature,
What tilth and pasture, path and orchard are,
The russet wall absorbing sun in summer,
The embracing firelight of the hall in winter
To forest folk who dread return of danger,
Gloating on barn and mill, they daily, gladly
Gave up their own dream to that dream, the stronger,
Whose bridle twitch was terror to the farmer
But struck into his soul, sweet compensation,
Love of a safe, harsh, iron domination.

3.

The grain soared upward into golden arches,
Transmuted into groined and pointed stone,
Miraculous vaulting, delicate great defiance
Of all the laws of earth; and men aspiring
To something better than law, beyond condition,
Tithe and toll, their poor bowed psyches soaring
Among these upward arches from the ground
Mingled with angels in melodious heights.
Other immortals had been at home on earth,
Bathed in rivers, hunted woods, chased girls
With womb and orifice, weak and wet to touch.
Now tempted to transcendence men became
Half-angels, monsters, who were soon to learn
How half-men hate the bodies which they mourn.

4.

Following the curve of arches, like a fountain,
The music of the mingled voices rose,
Seeming spontaneous, pure detached emotion.
The schemings that his fellows called ambition,
Conspiracies which served what passed for passion,
Furtive arrangements while with straight hair falling
Over his brow and level eyebrows, laughing
The loved one walked another line but knew him
Still for friend, lost in his soaring.
It seems to boys that spirit is a kingdom
Whose law is feeling, meeting like the arches.
They little know how marvellous calculation
Through which both note and arch meet in dependence.
But they will learn, and learn they are mistaken.

5.

Keeping his vigil nightlong in the chancel,
Seeing a vision of himself resplendent
Beside what gave him caste, his murderous weapons,
The always brave, the honourable one,
Sans peur et sans reproche, sought echo, answer
From something guiltless, sin-free but still human,
A virgin merging in her slender girlhood
With all which was appointed to confirm him
In his ideal of him. And as he knelt there
The hope grew unassuagable at last
Except by one so far above her fellows
That she could not be found, or, if found, taken,
Allow the peaks and valleys of her body
To be the territory of his hands.
Thus forfeited their friendship and their love.

6.

Leaving aside then for all time the songs
So wonderfully waiting to be sung
On that lost, long, tolling Sunday when he knew
So well the infinite bitterness of being young;
Leaving out break of cloud and depth of sky,
The green of water in a wooded place,
The answering curve of the always indomitable
Blood towards body's grace;
Leaving for ever out of dream and living
The beauty of the gravely mocking face;
What else remains to be remembered,
Or ever for time's remembrance to be said,
Before on the homely pillow of white death
He lays his tired with longing, mortal head?

7.

He rode to war along the rime-rimmed roads,
Awaiting wounds to prove his love for her,
His horse hooves splitting ice like sparkling stars.
And she was present like the evening star,
Like God or conscience, knowing all he did,
As he spoke nightly of his deeds to her,
Who saw him, careless, brave and generous,
As he, a hero in his own song, saw;
Who trembled for his daring as he dashed
Forward where danger was all but death.
And in this docile comradeship of hers,
Worshipping lance and badge and saddle straightness,
He found more than he would find, coming home
To that passivity he had wished upon her.

8.

But in that longing sweetness greater than
The sweetness sex released into the blood
When he rode south to Barbary where girls
Hung ripe as fruit and palpable and many.
Her absent presence was as light as air,
Like fountain spray, blown suddenly to stroke,
An amulet, a password or a charm.
So that when he returned and she was given
Unbrided, a mere mortal in the house,
An animal in bed, kind, egocentric,
No centre but periphery of space,
Aching for absence still he sought another
Whose beauty would be hedged by swords and forests
So the keen longing would go on forever.

9.

The arming and departure of the knights:
A picture by Burne-Jones in Birmingham.
The armourers are maidens clothed in white,
Cool draperies denying horse-hot limbs.
They raise their lashes to their lads, the knights,
Are almost bold in promise as they hand
The spear and shield, the sword and helmet up
That when he comes back, glory work all done,
The union he will find will be complete,
Demure but total, ending adolescent
Agonies, new manhood's long self doubtings,
Weakness acknowledging its opposite,
For strength reserving servile adoration:
Burne-Jones, a man, is painting a male dream.

10.

In the long fields he saw the woman crawl,
Hoeing and snagging, buttocks high, and took them
In that position when the steward brought them,
Naked of woollen cloth and washed as never
Since their day of birth in smoky cabins,
Blushing like roses or like russet apples.
Como un perro, laughed and forced his member
Between the labia, the strong thrust driving
The head, turned sideways, hair in disarray,
Among the rushes of the castle chamber.
Looking along the plane of back, the neck bared,
Saw just enough of face to savour dominance.
Como un perro. But it was the human
Against which he blasphemed, and not the animal.

11.

And when they knelt before him, took his member
Between their lips, their lashes low, allowing
Unquestioning prerogative, he suffered
Division in his heart. No ruler ever,
No owner of the women in the woods
While making free in search of his own pleasure
Dreamed girlhood set so strangely high above him,
So wished its blinding snows immaculate.
Torn thus could not find his delight with equals,
Dismayed by women of the kitchen aching
With lust just like his own, but liberal, human,
Preferred to dominate and found instead
Intoxicating stranger and much stronger
In knowing it was always an offence.

12.

The king sits, you will notice, fully armoured,
Impregnable in iron, while the maid
Is wearing just a shift or flimsy nightdress
Which clings to belly curve and even navel,
Shining, like, oddly, some post-war synthetic,
Her arms and shoulders very white and bare.
She's almost on an altar, perched above him,
He's practically kneeling down below,
Taking a good long look. Her gaze is fixed
On the wall behind him and above his head.
(Some never look at all at the front rows.)
'The meaning of it has been much debated.'
The female is a goddess to be worshipped.
Also an object you can sit and look at.

13.

Lady Burne-Jones thought that 'Cophetua'
Showed the special qualities of her husband's art
Better than anything else he ever painted.
Certainly steps and throne are deeply pleasing,
In their recessive quality at least.
It's said the girl is a Miss Francis Graham,
With whom he was in love, but who got married.
He's 'gazing at her in mute admiration.'
He had that curious garment specially made
And posed another model in it too.
The grave, sad face of course is still Miss Graham's.
That dear one can be worshipped like an icon
And placed, a precious object, on a shelf.
The shift reveals though. Equally the armour.

14.

The heather gives off sweetness in the warm
Impulsive air and over it hangs bee song
Like a cloud. Below, bright yellow furze
Crumbles dry rock; then the rich grass begins.
A river rubs its way past small clay cliffs
And inlets where sweet cattle sniff the water.
A silver bell is tolling. Holy men
Murmur a chant like bees. In outhouses
The women knead the bread, their creamy thoughts
Curl gently at the edges like the dough.
There is no history here, the hurt who make it
Banished to knife-sharp islands where they punish
Their sex for its impossible demands,
Rejections of this possible content.

15.

An air which softens outlines, blurs horizons,
Hides mountain ranges until suddenly
The black peaks soar, steep, huge and sodden over
A valley where the stream and road are one.
In this land nothing's clear, no colour sharp
Except the green. The browns and reds and purples
Change constantly and quickly with the moisture
Content of the air, as does the light.
The twilight lingers, bright but shadowless
Beyond the sunset. Since the sea surrounds
The whole, east light and west, north light and south
Are at the mercy of its mirror mass.
The south is sometimes clearer than the north
And ambiguity a law of life.

16.

The chief a hero and the herd boy kinsman
Hung on his gestures, watched his debonair
Way with a sword hilt, eagerly crouched and honoured
His hunger's empathy with the hillside's life.
And when the clan was summoned to the sign,
The high notes swelling in sweet auguries
Of fellowship and sacrifice, he followed
Until the day when all was lost and loyalty
Became the only riches to be shared.
He sat all night beside the sleeping form,
Lochiel wrapped in his cloak, his blonde, damp, royal
Hair on the heather's pillow. In the boy's full heart
A gratitude for service greater than
The systems know, or women, or even knowledge.

17.

Connolly wrote that all was held in common,
That everyone was equal in the clan,
Copying Mrs Alice Stopford Green,
As did the whole intoxicated crew.
There was no competition. None could fail.
For boys confirmed what Scott and Stevenson
Had said of something other than a world
In which each little family looked out
From narrow windows on their enemies,
Plotting advantage like conspirators.
MacNeill put a stop to that in 1912,
Gave Russell a breakdown, upset the rest.
MacNeill, 'that traitor', but a scholar too.
All scholarship is perhaps a kind of treason.

18.

Such lived by litheness, by the quick reflex,
The lunge and limit of the lovely claw,
So lazy but so terrible in stroke,
Their tawniness the only value known,
Until the law, an awe-struck lover, gave
The sanction of the temple and the grove,
The exactitudes of language and its grace
To pre-existing power and privilege.
They now had all, arched foot and architecture,
The woods within whose wildness they still hunted,
The earth which they had seized and wedded like
A cataclysm in the long ago.
So more than natural seemed, so weak they were,
Surpassing nature, ignorant of its ways,
And ignorant too of number, interest.

19.

And suddenly their limbs grew weak, their weapons
Awkward and wayward in their gauche right hands.
From the smoke-shrouded city which had sheltered
So much that was unmentionable: plague,
Curiosity, measurement, foreign women,
Emerged a strange miasma, whose effect
On them was as infection, though the ones
About whom as a magic or a cloud
It hung, seemed unaffected, even strengthened.
When such came with this aura and calm eyes
Ancient woods withered at the very root,
The land, their bride, turned alien and cold.
Strange mist which tainted all that they thought good
And yet enhanced too everything men owned.

20.

More shocking than the westward sea being blocked,
The discovery that all was now for sale.
Many had understood how brutish power
Could overbear, entrap the bright and brave,
Bring the slight trembling virgin to the bed,
Send statuary crashing to the ground,
Reduce the Lord's anointed to a wretch
Pleading for pardon or a sup of water.
Still there was honour, which could be lost, suborned,
But not sold like a chattel to another,
Fidelity, forever a fixed star,
Entitlement, a wine within the blood,
And field and wood entailed to son and heir.
Strange they should think the sale of these the worst.

21.

Le Roi Soleil, the great sun burning down
On all his subjects, brought a sort of light.
He cut the finest figure in the world
On his high heels with ribbons at his knees.
And he built nobly too. The oxen dragged
Long carts through rutted clay, boards buckling under
Huge blocks of stone until the architect's
Conception rose, baroque and beautiful.
All this was quite gratuitous, a fountain
Is not a dour necessity of state;
And though the powerful hydraulic pumps
Which he commissioned are still marvels, they
Were not employed except in the king's garden's
So those free from necessity invent.

22.

The boredom was extreme. The lack of privacy
Unbearable. He went to bed in public
And ate his breakfast under the crowd's stare.
The closet lined with books and ledgers, sex
Like a shameful contract between two,
These were inventions of the bourgeoisie.
They played cards endlessly, intrigued and gossiped,
Screaming inside with rage like idle children,
Hour after hour, talk, talk; and, worse still, wit.
Gallantry was a task required, exacted.
And only war provided work of import,
Almost as stern as that the bourgeois did.
'O Richard, *o mon roi*', the royalists
Would sing, invoking sweet recovered dangers.

23.

The Great Crown was surmounted by a Cross.
The judge twitched ermine and adjusted scarlet.
The archbishop's purple matched his purple lips.
Insignia and symbol proved the man
Himself but instrument, though with a taste
For blood, or boys, or beauties kept like deer
Within a park. The mob outside the gates
Saw symbol first; of God's power greater than
The human office, but that greater than
The mortal man who filled it. Blows at this
Struck at the ceremony of the universe,
Stars in melodic courses, high on high,
Not at poor privilege, thin-shanked and trembling,
Keeping with fear his darlings, strange as deer.

24.

The classic portico confronts the lake
Flung like a challenge to its very steps.
The inspirational, instinctual,
Flees like the deer to forest and green fern.
We put our trust in clearer definition,
Contract and construct, law and well marked limit,
Reason proclaiming all mankind was one,
Its interests symmetrical and known,
The set square, T square and dividers could
Map out its future on a drawing board.
Masters who made possessions the sole order
Twisted the reasoning. Rebellious, sullen,
Native to darkness now, the instincts gathered,
Hate in their hearts and hateful in their turn.

25.

O blessed fruits of hate, unthinking hate,
Unknowing, without theory or even
Without cause, the smouldering, sullen hate
Of peasants grimed from birth, grimed in the bone,
Who know themselves inferior for ever
Who can never even stroll like him in gardens
Never be free in body or with bodies,
Or pause like him at the apex of the dance.
Hate the last holy, inextinguishable
Prerogative of those too cowardly
Ever to strike a blow, who shamble by
In humble silence while the horsemen pass,
Their secret flame, their pledge and proud distinction,
Their sole assertion of an opposite state.

26.

Their ancestors were wise, they dug and trenched,
Plumbing foundations in the quaking soil.
Raising the chaste, severe and classical
Column, entablature and pediment,
Reproving nature with proportion's stare
And showing man a measure for joy.
So let stand thus forever stylobate,
Podium, portico and collonade,
Organic artlessness acknowledged in
The thin acanthus leaf but now transcended.
Who tumbles, burns or tarnishes beware
How rare is balance, brought about in mass,
Rightness which none can rectify, dispute,
The threatened made enduring, lines in air.

27.

But strike they did and threw a king's cropped head
As gage of battle to the kings of Europe,
Thus horrifying many gentle souls.
And Erba said, a far day to remember,
Walking beside Max Reinhardt's urns and columns,
Two suns, the second broken on the water,
Schloss Leopold, the joy of the baroque,
A tracery across the darker side,
No Barbara that day; 'Unhappiness
Came into Europe with that revolution
As mode where only misery had been.'
Through thirty years quite clear, two poets in amber.
Now after all those years I find the answer:
No, not unhappiness but discontent.

28.

Sweet Liberty enthroned in Notre Dame,
A smudged girl, carmined, licking nervous lips.
The wits joked, as she tremulously mounted,
Her lath and plaster eminence of mounts
And the innumerable clients who had climbed them.
Thus Liberty and Whoredom rose together
And have been quite inseparable since,
Freedom to prostitute themselves enjoyed
By talented persons in all walks of life
And money able to command young minds,
Their willingness, their grace, their sober virtue.
Contract instead of status it's been called.
Executives in Saabs who know their worth,
Smarter of course than other kinds of whore.

29.

And Emmet said, his voice a dulcet tenor,
'I placed a time bomb under the Free State,
It was one of my sneered-at technical devices,
My exploding cobble-stones and signal rockets,
"When my country takes her place among the nations,
Then and not till then…" You know the gist.
They cut off my head when they cut me up in Thomas Street,
A mess of offal, thrown to political dogs,
Yet I had been clever for once, in spite of my blunders.
Cosgrave at mass in a morning coat, winged collar,
Could hear beyond the coughing and the gabble
The beat of a Jacobin drum. We were both politicians.
Is it not the Jacobin dream that is scrawled in the jacks:
"Up the Republic. Up the IRA."?'

30.

'They dragged the Lord Chief Justice from his coach,
A mottled and blanched old man who loved his grandchild.
This has been held against me ever since
Alike by those who say, what is, is right,
And those who say what is not should remain
With unstained annals until it becomes
The true republic, Roman, rational.
My superbly folded stock and flowered waistcoat,
The justice and humanity of my cause,
My acquaintance with the works of Paine and Rousseau,
Worthless, in face of this. Yet this was progress.
Your other sad rebellions had been raised
For rural reasons. Mine at least were modern.
My mob was European, avant-garde.'

31.

'I was ignorant of tribal rights and wrongs,
Sad wranglings over scrub and bog, the rival
Interpretation of the books of wrath,
And cared not much for nations either except
As communes with accountable delegates.
Doubtless, though, many who followed me may have wanted
Some sort of mystic justice or reversal.
To see a fine old gentleman shitting his breeches
And hear him cry for absent law and order.
Of course there were human passions outside my range.
They were not all on the level of dreamy Dowdall,
Quigley and bricklayer, learned Stafford the baker,
But I took what was a hand in the real world,
The hatreds it creates, its judges foster.'

32.

Almost as if they had a horror of
The things we find consoling to the spirit,
The rook-filled trees around the rectory,
The restless sighing of the captive with the leaves,
The river's ceaseless conflict stones,
The weeping cattle, clustered at the gate,
And the rich fields, the rippling flanks of earth,
They fled their rose-embowered dwellings for
The deserts of uprooting, a new landscape,
Poisoned, where nothing grew and even sky
Was man-made, black as coal, where, hope abandoned,
Of any sign that what they saw intended
A destiny for them in harmony
With nature, they now thronged through the great gates.

33.

But nature too had now been touched by man,
It's very root and branch, each berry, tuber,
The shining blades of grass, the bleating sheep
Who spread like an infection through the vales,
The golden ears of corn, which, bursting through
Had once asserted that the scheme of things
Was constant in its bargain with the earth,
Now advertised from every slope and hillside
A new exclusion, worse than frosts of winter:
Tongued in the trees, writ in the running brooks,
The law of contract and of property.
The horror of their hunger, so reflected
Even by burnished mirrors of rich corn
Was what they fled from in dumb multitudes.

34.

When mothers in the dark courts off the Strand
Were grateful to their scarcely visible stars
They had a girl to sell that some gent wanted;
And it became a public nuisance that
Whole herds escaped from sweat shops filled Haymarket
And Regent Street right up to Oxford Circus;
When in the *haut monde*, in the highest, best
Circles of all it was well understood
That wives, the ones a man would think worth having
Were bought, then made, the bourgeois thought it shocking.
The writers re-invented virtue and
Wept at the loss of it by these fallen angels.
Prostitute was a word of feminine gender.
What they did in the world was not for money.

35.

Surprised to find Heine died at fifty-nine,
So brave a soldier lasting out that long.
With Byron the first of the open-necked shirt brigade,
Breast bared to bullets and a songster's throat.
A lawyer too and took the full degree,
Which does not mean that he knew any laws
Except the ones we all know, heart and home,
Inertia, conscience, two and two make four
And one are three, old self-hood working out
A destiny in conflict with much else,
And, in his case, consumption of the spine.
Of course his German Jewish friend would work
On the harsh laws of history, instruct
Heine, who once had heard Napoleon's drums.

36.

Those graves in Père Lachaise. We saw his too,
A humble soldier in the eternal war,
My felon friend and I, a lawyer, as
He later was to charge. Yes, guilty as…
We sat where Liberty spread her skirts on gravel,
The box smell stronger in the heat of France
Mingled with wine fumes as we toasted him,
A lawyer without law, a rebel tradesman.
The birds in the black cypress tree nearby
Sang doubtless of sweet liberty as once
They had in Wexford, in the song at least.
Heine was pensioned by the French, such freedom
From everything except the lower back
Consumption and the Jewish pull, ours Irish.

37.

These liberation soldiers, born too early,
And some, like poets after Pound, not learning
That things had changed, as Heine's friend insisted.
Liberty, like all goddesses, could vanish
When you got up too close. She was the rocks,
The mountains and the sea, she was the storm.
Still freedom, still, thy banner, torn but flying
Streams like a thundercloud against the wind.
She wasn't Austria, she wasn't priesthood,
In Shelley's case at least she wasn't vows.
Odd, though she pre-supposed for most some money, they
Did not connect her absence with the absence
Of cash, which could abrogate priests, vows, archdukes.
Rich liberals in Florence with their wives.

38.

For some she was colours on the map, not fast.
While Garibaldi's rebels fought, Cavour
Took in what dirty linen was on offer.
Triumph of red meant that in the piazza
Liquid Italian flowed, the Hapsburg Duke
Fled baggageless, escorted by his Austrians,
A wheel gone spinning down the slope, the abyss.
Funds in the bank no doubt with the freemasons
Finding a new relationship with bankers too,
As well they might, who now ran the Departments,
Rich peasants renting, but, the olive ripe,
Would rob and squeeze mere labourers in a press.
Yes, liberty was great, except for those
Who needed her the most, poor absolutists.

39.

Hating the hill, the hollow and the stream,
Horizons that were given by the gods,
It was for end of Eden that he yearned.
Surrender to the natural was all
The village offered the divided, when
The girls lost innocence they were received
With eager moanings straight into the sweet
Circle of sense and animals shared too.
The little screams from down the river path
Echoed complicities in old wives' dreams.
They mumbled still of sin, but when he trembled
It was for something other than this joy,
A thought which merely followed the blood's curve,
As common springing as a wayside flower.

40.

All in the end were friends here, ruthless games
Ended with lovers proved their clemency.
The treacherous wrestlings in the orchard grass,
The thunder of the heavy days in May,
The ponderous couplings of the callous beasts
Bore smiling innocence like crops that were
Blessed by the parsons at the harvest home.
The dawn in dark that was the city's glow,
The shining surfaces of its alleyways
Beckoned to strange complicities beyond
These happy minglings of opponent loves.
His breath stopped for the imminence of a place
Where all of Eden's terms would be reversed,
Love, hate, pain, pleasure wear each other's face.

41.

Baudelaire was 'out' in '48
When Buisson saw him at the barricades
With a double-barrelled gun and cartridge belt,
Both looted from the gun-shop round the corner.
He was crying wildly, 'Death to General Aupick',
But did not add he was the General's step-son.
Later in *My Heart Laid Bare* he listed
His motives as a revolutionary:
'The thirst for vengeance.'
Yes, we know that thirst.
'The natural pleasure taken in destruction.'
We know that also, our own hearts laid bare.
And lastly a more subtle one perhaps.
'The intoxication brought about by reading.'
Yes, revolution is a bookish pastime.

42.

He persuaded Champfleury to call their paper
'*Le Salut Public*'. The name recalled
Deliberately the Committee of the Terror.
'The violent and abnormal had a deep
Attraction for him', someone else records.
Alas the normal soon came back again.
After the hot June days the barricades
Were swept away like remnants of a fête.
Order, as many called it, was restored.
Large numbers wanted peace. He too perhaps.
'The patron saint of rebels is old Nick;
And Revolution was "the Antichrist".'
'When I consent to be republican
I commit evil knowingly', he wrote.

43.

Yet he was there. He made the synthesis
Between the consciousness of one's own sins,
One's sweat of soul, one's dubious private motives
And the clear merits of the public cause,
Beckoning like a bath to cool and clean.
If only those whose motives were quite pure
And hearts quite free from hatred could cast stones
Or root up cobbles for a barricade
It would be a lonely business, revolution.
No-one suggests the cohorts of reaction
Should be so free from the original
Stain as the ones who want a different world.
Indeed their stock-in-trade is to know all
The twistings and deceits of greed and lust
And make good use of them in daily business.

44.

Only the working class might still be loved,
Who toiled and died of white lead poisoning,
Hated the rich consistently, like Christs,
For only they were somehow still above him,
Gave him example in their suffering,
Could even be his heroes. They were soldiers
In a holy war against the virtuous,
The moral order of the bourgeois world,
Whose basis, as he knew, was prostitution,
Pleasing alike to prostitute and client.
Their servitude alone was not self-chosen
With wiles and grace, vile hypocrisies,
If they did not exist, proud victims in their hovels,
He would be alone, like Satan, in denial.

45.

Amid the roar of iron-hooped wheels on cobbles,
The rush of narrow shoulders through those streets,
Where ghosts by day accosted passers-by
And memories weighed heavier than stones;
Or at evening when sad whores and clients prowled
Seeking to sell revenge or buy it cheap,
There would be no place at all for such as he.
At home where cat and mistress gazed in cold
Uncomprehending savagery at the coals;
In theatres where women's eyes reflected
The icy centre of the chandelier;
With spleen and glee contending in his heart
He would know the double exile: he from them
And they and he together from the Garden.

46.

At country girls who caught their breath in wonder
Along the boulevard the lights winked back.
She worried in the wash-house steam about
The skin that bared would one day please the wankers
And, given a bit of luck, a rich protector.
Lautrec apotheosised her, made her crudeness
Tawdry no longer through intensity
As, stony faced, she danced her sad defiance
Of propriety or modesty or that
Innate sense of a woman's place in things,
Shy, virgin, fearful and a man's invention
Which all had brought from villages to lose,
Which men destroy and recreate and hope
In pervert hearts will still be there to use.

47.

The laundry left at last, her red-armed comrades
Joking in the steam, her name in lights now,
La Goulue was a star for five good years,
But then began to drink. Though Lautrec came
And Oscar and the famous Feneon
To see her as a fairground novelty,
The face grew coarse, lost line as well as charm.
Her nerve ends screaming in the fat for drink
She shared a stinking cage with starving lions
And rolling like a mountain round the ring
Wrestled opponents of her own weak sex.
The bored crowd drifted by to find some other
Mockery of what womanhood had been
Once, back where they had come from and their mothers.

48.

Girls on the river, girls at Argenteuil,
Under the dappling trees in August light,
Skirts full and creamy like cloth waterfalls
Brushing the grass, each ankle an example
Of how athletic angels are, as eager
They stepped on land at one of Sunday's stages.
The light declines at last. The dance begins
And music mingles with the wine in veins
Alive to summer and condemned to Monday.
Passion like night may follow light's decline
And be at odds with openness of glance.
Which should have lasted longer. We could ask
Was the whole day as easy as it seems,
Their comradeship unclouded like the moon?

II

49.

What was it like in the Garden? As naked as birch trees,
Their skin as native as sight as sheen of the river,
The curve of buttock but as the curve of bole,
No cloth occluding its shock or smooth synthetics,
To cling, suggest, to ruck and to reveal?
And psyches without disguise or covering either,
Everything natural, instinctive, happy,
No kinks, no hang-ups and no fetishes,
No thought thought daring, or no thought at all.
It may have been a munch, but Baudelaire
Would not have been at home there, nor, in truth,
Might you, o hypocrite *lecteur*, less hypo-
Ocrite perhaps, more hip than them,
Those clear-eyed innocents in unshadowed grove.

50.

And one presumes equality. Of course.
Which wouldn't be like Milton, that's for sure,
Since he's quite clear about the dominance.
'Not equal as their sex not equal seemed;
For contemplation he and valour formed,
For softness she and sweet attractive grace;
He for God only, she for God in him.
His fair large front and eye sublime declared
Absolute rule.' It would not do today,
At least in theory, though old Adam might
Still get a bit of what he got, which was
'Subjection, but required with gentle sway,
And by her yielded, by him best received
Yielded, with coy submission, modest pride
And sweet, reluctant, amorous delay.'

51.

One likes that second yielded: 'by him best
Received/yielded.' His weight in other words
Not thrown about, but still some let's pretend
She didn't want to . . . what? Oh well, whatever.
A little later on we're told that they
Being spared – 'eased' is in fact the word –
The putting off of clothes (and underclothes?)
'Those troublesome disguises which we wear'
(Sweet catches, strippings, stages and delays)
'Straight side by side were laid; nor turned, I ween,
Adam from his fair spouse, nor Eve the rites
Mysterious of connubial love refused.'
Make what you like of that 'mysterious'.
And, since we're at it, of that 'nor … refused'.

52.

But female sexuality is not
Somehow a thing that seems to trouble him
In spite of his three wives. The impression is
Of love and duty happily performed.
Blind he could never see the drawn-back lips,
The teeth tips bared in that sweet ecstasy,
So sweet for the beholder, holder too.
Yet if he loved their womanhood as well
As his own masculinity, or loved
A different image of himself as male,
He sought, no doubt in darkness, love perhaps,
Those shudderings and that fierce abandonment,
His keen ear heard those cries, which, puritans
Of their own pleasure though men are, redeem.

53.

May not of course have found them, like so many,
Even most perhaps, tale all too sad to tell
And told too often in the marriage bed.
De Sade knew all about the clitoris.
Freud didn't, not at least in 1912.
Ms Carter in 'The Sadean Woman' says
The eighteenth century aristocrat
('Lecher' but I must keep my iambic beat)
'Knew that manipulation of the clitoris
Was the unique (sic) key to the female orgasm…
That this grand simplicity was all there was
To the business.' Sade could learn.
Although a doctor the good bourgeois couldn't.
Knowledge is power, yes, but power is knowledge.

54.

But men they say had power, while women lay
In darkness through the ages. It's more likely,
Most thought it bully just to keep their nerve
And take their pleasure and be somewhat thankful,
Subjection but required with gentle sway,
Being, as Milton said, the best to aim at.
Of course most women were as ignorant
About themselves as any man could be
And so no tender whisperings at all
Could put things right, if any thought them wrong.
Millions believed that they were simply frigid.
Some thought that they were the odd woman out.
Lighten that darkness, Lord, let our time flower,
A rose whose opening is still full of wonder.

55.

Our fathers must have lain there in the darkness,
Candle ends guttering and the sweet dreams fled,
Imagining if that union could not be
That there could be no other in their garden.
Was it our fathers who lay there in darkness,
Watching the dawn come, dry-eyed now at last,
While marriage stretched before them like a life?
Or did our mothers all, like whores, pretend
Cheerfully sometimes, even, wretchedly
At others, or decide it did not matter?
Perhaps it was a class thing, as most may be.
You brought pretence or blithely did without it,
Secure in your own excellence and worth,
Or equally secure in ignorance.

56.

The early waves of western travellers
Caressed with envious eyes the glittering skins
Beneath the fern fronds, saw free-loving peoples
Made careless by ripe marrows of the morrow.
Paul Gauguin, burdened similarly with work
He didn't want to do, a wife who was
A complex history, longed like lecherous sailors
To share in such simplicities and be
A noble savage free of past and future.
It didn't quite work out. He brought with him
His absolutes and silly contradictions.
He sought the modern in the innocent,
Sought love with spirochetes in his blood,
Asked answers to the questions posed in Paris.

57.

The lower middle classes still believed
There never could be much and that much worked for.
And even the romantics were quite certain
It could not buy the things that really mattered
The steady grey-eyed gaze of understanding,
Time waiting on a leaf in autumn woods,
The envied love of enviable women.
One hardly needs to add that he missed out on
Much that was merely a short drive away,
A passing taxi or a routine flight.
Journey they must if lovers will have meetings.
Nor do the happy ask when they have landed,
Why money like the ocean drowns all guilt,
Why the shore smiles on those who have attained it.

58.

It took five centuries to know for sure
That it was really so. The nobs adjusted,
Not without trauma, but as nobs will do;
And though we've heard about the *trahison
Des clercs* as if that sin was something new,
The fact is that the clerks knew all about
The sale of their poor goods a while before
The buyability of everything
Became accepted as a law of life.
(The author of the Rosetta Stone, a liar
Twice over, whether needfully or not,
Wrote, 'Ptolemy, ever living, loved by Piah').
No, it was common people who believed
The hierarchical lies which still remain.

59.

A handy weapon in the hands of those
Whose business was confusion. Finance now
In league with aristocracy, priesthood,
Conservativism of all kinds to pretend
The guiding principle of the world was not
How much it's worth, but whether it's worthwhile
And worthy and worth doing and of worth
In sight of man and God. Even Dickens's poor
Swallowed it with their gruel. Though the desperate
Might be benumbed past caring and the sly
Might have caught on quite quickly to the game
There were poor honest workmen in this century
Who suffered disillusionment as great
As first war soldiers finding their betters out.

60.

Quite common people, stubborn in their faith
As Kitchener's footsloggers, still believing
Long after it was known as lunacy
By all their lords and masters, that the world
Was by and large a place where one was called
To do some service, honourably and well.
The clerks – another sort of clerk –
In Pim's believed the ledgers could not lie:
You gave good value and the books would show it.
An eye for the fast buck and the quick kill,
The railroad millionaires, Jay Gould and Rockefeller,
Manipulating governments and trusts,
As foreign to their ethos if they knew
As later would be poor diseased Capone.

61.

City of dreams the tenors sang, the Danube,
Grey in the rain had veiled itself in blue.
The powerful were like children dressing up
In plumes and bear-skins, thigh high boots and breastplates,
Their children garbed like sailors come ashore.
It was the baroque, sustaining itself on disguise.
Even the buildings wore epaulettes like generals.
Of course what they wore off duty was formal also.
When hierarchs went out on the town to sample
The pleasures of the flesh they wore top hats
And opera cloaks with red or purple lining.
As in the novels and the melodramas
The toff could be a murderer or a king.
Only the poor were clearly seen as such.

62.

At the salon an over-dressed crowd saw Klimt had bared
One breast of an over-dressed model and found it shocking.
But the totally naked did not seem natural either.
The nudes of Egon Schiele were not rosy like Renoir's
Reclining, rejoicing in their own fleshly nature.
They were skinny children, stripped, at a disadvantage,
Sometimes resenting, challenging the gaze.
Karl Kraus said the Empire lived by the art of the drape.
The oppressor covers up and strips at will.
The victims loathe their own sad bodies most.
Of course there was Adolf Loos whose simple buildings
'Well-formed and comely in the nude', he said,
Would augur a new age of nakedness.
Still Schiele's girls sulk, are brassy or just sad.

63.

The body into which the soul was sent
Cringing from the gaze, assessment, inquisition,
Has unclean parts and functions, shameful, nameless
Intensely conscious of itself but lacking
A happy sense of self as natural object,
Weaker than others, always vainly grasping,
Impotent as a jug of slopped out water,
Uncertain, imprecise in reach and compass
Recalcitrant alike to will and impulse,
A mere inadequate vehicle for wish,
Its many failures making imprecision
And approximation its habitual modes.
It was not the body's passions which dismayed
The soul but its unworthiness for love.

64.

These were the modern things. One spoke of Schoenberg,
Hoffmannsthal, Rilke, Kaiser, Stefan George.
The Secession was, as you might say, well-established.
One argued about Freud and knew that Mach
Had at last rid science of metaphysical ghosts.
It was really only ill-bred schoolmasters,
Post office clerks, Slavonic mysticists,
Those ill at ease in our great German culture
And politicians on the make who spoke
At boring length about what they would call
The problem of the nationalities.
And yet you know they made this jejune topic
Somehow the burning issue, though even the Marxists
Laughed at them. They did. They really did.

65.

With skill the slabs were blasted and then split
For billiard-table tops. The smooth slate sang
In harmony with the ivories, permanent, heavy
As rich Havana clinging to beige and curtains.
Now in the cavern which the quarrying left
Noticing the resemblance to a famous grotto
The parish priest has placed an electric virgin.
Six hundred yards from here the cable rose
Seaweed hung from the depths. Such hawsers bound
The new world to the old, Wall Street to waggish men
Bent over cues and cunts. A miracle
Is needed to restore the pristine wonders,
The stage-door Johnnies' joys, expanding markets,
The simple faith of villages and islands.

66.

In 1901 Marconi sent
Across the wastes a more ethereal message.
While Chesterton on the 9.15 regretted
Dying romance and blamed Lloyd George, the jews,
Moustaches ticked thighs as white as ivory
And gents and mashers hunted the same game.
The ether grew more bodeful, fleets assembled
Off stormy headlands hissed the stokers' fires.
The Boys Own Paper went to bed to taps.
Romance persisted, even on the Somme.
One morning as old Europe's sun brought dawn,
A quarryman who was placing charges would
Look at the vibrant sky and see come in
A monoplane irradiate with rain.

67.

In Russia suffering is preached as a mode of salvation.
The poor are seen as martyrs, sometimes envied.
Mere endurance is sanctified by religion.
Our writing glorifies misunderstanding and pain.
Lenin rejected all this. I have never known
A human being so possessed by hatred
Of all forms of unhappiness and grief,
Suffering and want as he was. Yes, he had
A burning faith that none of them were essential
And unavoidable parts of human life
But abominations that we should regard as such
And could bring an end to. It was very striking
His vision of a snow bright, sunlit world,
Empty of ache, disappointment, hunger, sorrow.

68.

But even supposing that most formal crime
Was, as reformers said, a product of
Environment and sprouted from the dark
Sad walls of tenements or bread in parlours
With aspidistra plants; and further say
Our selfish and familiar agonies,
Ambition, envy, disappointed love,
Were gone like greed from human life somehow,
One wonders what of moral suffering,
The consciousness of wrong-doing, the ache
Of other lives in ours, of conscience like
A spectre with us in the noonday sun?
It's either that we'd do no wrong or be
Vultures in sunlight, picking the bone clean.

69.

Internalised self-punishment perhaps,
The super-ego battering on the head
Of the old harmless ego, just another
Of the notorious drawbacks we have bought
In swapping our old paradises of
The happy instincts, dancing on the beach,
After a day of murder and before
Some rough stuff fucking in the plaintain groves,
Whatever plaintains are, or mangrove swamps
Supposing you can fuck in mangrove swamps.
Yes, civilisation has its discontents,
But still there are objective wrongs, objective
Balances we're called up to strike.
The rational vultures pick the eyes out first.

70.

Matisse had painted lovely nudes reclining
In joyous being, *Le Bonheur De Vivre*.
When he went to dinner with Miss Stein and Leo
He would see his rival's lyric painting there.
And of course he'd also seen the other one,
Luxe Calme et Volupté, the centrepiece
Of the autumn salon a few months before.
Comparisons with Ingres were freely made:
'A pagan joy'. 'The deep well spring of life'.
He would paint some nudes. One night in Avinyo
A girl with heavy, sullen features squatting
Before a sailor with her cunt pulled wide,
Her back to us, beside her on the table
Anther joyful fruit, a split, pink melon.

71.

The other demoiselles stand round about,
Accessible as melons on a table,
Their bodies savagely distorted, faces
Horribly expressionless, blank-eyed,
But posing in mechanic attitudes
Of provocation, joylessly assumed,
Routinely, to arouse mechanic lust.
The sailor is gone now, we are in the centre,
As brute as any mariner with money,
The squatting woman's head is twisted towards us,
A savage mask, dull, ochreous, diabolic.
'You paint as if you want us all to drink
Petrol and eat rope ends,' Braque was to say
As penitential Spain proclaimed the modern.

72.

Marinetti went to see the guns.
Oiled steel recoiling. Plume. The answering puff
Among the crumbling terraces was death.
This was at Adrianople, 1912.
He had to prove a point, the only hygiene
Of the dirty world was war, and prove as well
That engines ran the show. Well, so they did.
With screaming gears the lorries brought the brave.
The Bulgars laid a railway down, the line
Blighting the orange groves. All except mules
And men was spherical, rectangular,
The ribbed skin of the flying machine composed
Of interpenetrating planes, its prop
A perfect arc. Severini would be pleased.

73.

'M. Bleriot has guided a plane in a given direction
Over the strip of sea that makes England an island
And under not too favourable conditions.
What the French aviator can do in 1909
A thousand aeroplanes can do in five years time.
When Farman flew a mile it was possible to say
An ingenious new toy had been invented.
A machine which can fly the channel is not a toy.
It is a deathly instrument of war'.
The *Times* was wrong. The instruments of war
Are toys and toys remain till death do part.
With fixed guns firing through the Farman's blades
It was a schoolboy honour they redeemed,
Released into the infinite at last.

74.

In the summer twilight thousands filled the streets,
Embracing, weeping, eyes and faces shining.
And then as darkness fell there came the singing,
The old heart-breaking songs, the mighty, soaring
En braust ein Ruf wie Donnerhall and after
The stern strong hym of German Protestants,
Ein' feste Burg ist unser Gott. I moved
Slowly along the Wilhelmstrasse with them.
It was as if I floated with the crowds,
Forgetful now of self, immersed like them
In a great tide of Germanness, of oneness.
Although what was to come was terrible
That night seems still august, magnificent.
I shiver when I think of it today.

75.

How sad the bugle in the wood's green depths
Aching for what is lost now to the world,
Least told of all tales now, least sung of songs
Since on those summer roads the marching boys
Sang out between the poplars in their dream
Of death in some great circumstance of friends,
Some proof of love beyond the dull demands
They never had expected, made each dawning
Among the little houses, little streets,
Between the window and the door of bedrooms,
In offices where courage was submission,
Where duty was a dragging chain and sacrifice
A grim sad burden carried to the end,
No bugle sounding, even for the brave.

76.

Hate was in short supply, as were munitions,
And needed to be mass-produced like them.
'I hate not Germans,' Edward Thomas wrote,
And he was typical in that of many.
Until Lord Northcliffe found the right imago.
Self-images were stronger. In imagination
A valorous self had waited which could be
Ardent, magnanimous and chivalrous,
Could prove itself at last a schoolboy's hero.
And it was strange how as the nations parted,
Their promontories reaching for each other,
Their shore lights vanishing beneath dark seas,
They were united in their knightly yearnings
As they had never been by saner visions.

77.

When I took the train my work was thoroughly abstract.
In the years before I had been, as I thought, liberated,
But at the front, without any break at all
I found myself among real, intractable things
And the men who worked with them every day of their lives,
My companions in the engineering corps,
Miners, drivers, workers in metal and wood.
On my first day there I was dazzled by the breech
Of a seventy-five, a gun which was standing uncovered
In the August sun, the magic of light on white metal.
This was enough to make me forget abstraction,
The art of nineteen twelve was dead for me.
Once I had fallen in love with that kind of reality
I was never again released from actual objects.

78.

In those first months of the war he grew quite thin.
The skull, which has always been near, showed clearly through.
Although at Cracow after Krasnin he
Had seen the stretchers jostled through the crowds,
The dead laid out in rows, the women wailing,
He never spoke of war as suffering.
He would open newspapers eagerly and read
As if he were burning a hole in every page.
The gruff good nature those who knew him best
Had noted as his mode of intercourse
Vanished. He was quite impersonal.
Worse, when he read of some atrocious happening
He would burst out laughing. His amusement then
Seemed genuinely uncontrollable.

79.

They showed him to the special waiting room
Formerly used by the imperial family.
The welcoming committee stood about.
He clutched a presentation bunch of roses,
Unhappily, not knowing where to put it.
Then Cheikidze made a formal speech.
'The principle task,' he said, 'is to defend
The revolution which has been accomplished
Against attacks from within and from without.'
While he was speaking Lenin looked around,
Examining the ceiling and the walls
As though the sentiments he heard expressed
Did not concern him personally at all,
As though they welcomed someone else, not him

80.

Then he stepped forward, putting down his roses
And taking off his bowler hat. Ignoring
The people in the waiting room he spoke
Through the open door to the murmuring crowd beyond.
'The peoples' need is peace and land and bread.
They give you hunger, war and landlordism.
The revolution has been just begun.
It must end in total victory or perish.
You are the advance guard of that victory.
Long live the world revolution just begun.'
The committee was clearly uneasy at these words
But the soldiers now were presenting arms and the cheering
Was swelling under the roof of the station outside
To a great roar of joy and recognition.

81.

There were no lights outside except the searchlights
Which the Kronstadt sailors had brought from the Peter Paul.
These picked out the lettering, gold on big red banners.
The bands had begun to play 'the Marseillaise'.
They carried Ilyich to an armoured car.
He stood on the bonnet and spoke, repeating simply
What he'd already said to the crowd inside.
'This is the world revolution just begun.'
The cars then started for the Ksheninskaya.
Our headlights were the only ones full on.
In the beams we could see the guard of workers and soldiers
Stretching ahead on both sides of the road.
Those who have not lived through revolution
Can not imagine its great and solemn beauty.

82.

The time was ripe. At least they thought it was.
For the double helices of Tatlin's tower,
The dialectic process soaring upwards
In interlocking spirals, leaps and bounds.
In revolutions and catastrophes;
And ripe too for Lissitzky's Lenin tribune,
The leader over voids on leaning steel;
The Pravda building's bold transparency
Abolishing the concept of the wall;
The Workers' Palace with its outside girders,
Naked tension cables, ventilators,
Bridge and mass, riding on transience.
Whether the time was ripe or not it never
Will seem so in quite that way ever now.

83.

For these remained mere projects. Trotsky said
'I know that meetings need arenas but
These need not take the form of cylinders
And the cylinders need certainly not revolve.'
Lenin disliked most things that end in 'ism
And did not see how they were all connected.
That Dadaists in Zurich called themselves
'Conductors and condensers of the new',
The metaphor did not appeal although
Electrification plus the Soviets
Was now his definition of what next.
Stalin put gothic pinnacles on skyscrapers.
Sixty years later the Centre Pompidou
Proclaims the ripeness of another time.

84.

'The Council of Peoples Commissars resolves
That the monuments erected by the Tsars
Which have no historical or artistic value
Be removed at once from the streets and squares of our cities.
It is further instructed to mobilise the artists
To create maquettes of monuments which might
Be put in place of these abominations.'
Erase the past, said Marinetti too.
'Museums are cemeteries where old corpses rot
In hateful rows. Though one might like to make
An annual pilgrimage on All Souls's Day,
One should beware the poisons one might breathe.'
Pious commissars would have demurred.
They were concerned about artistic values.

85.

Although such forms astounded by their beauty,
Machines were innocent of beauty's claims.
Their mundane purposes had freed them from
The tyranny of ideal loveliness.
No fog of memory, remorse, regret
Clung to their clean, inhospitable surface;
And so men weakened by their women, mothers,
Priests and philosophers, ideals, honour,
Saw in their pounding shafts, their piston blows
Bright metaphors of what mankind could be
Freed from the mists and moonlight of the past.
Their metal hearts beat purposefully on,
Needing no visions, pledges, pacts with time.
For they were time and future, and time's pledge.

86.

Picabia at the wheel of a Bugatti,
The horn's bulb to his painterly right hand,
Peaked cap reversed like any Kerry hurler.
Strange opposites, but both sufficing myths.
And this was nearer than the Kerry hurlers,
A strapped-down bonnet and the dream of booting
Round Brooklands or along the Great North Road.
The lower middle class did not believe
There could be women like the mistresses
Who kept him in such cars though he ditched both.
And ditched poor modernism too, to make a trio.
A member of the lower middle class
Would never reckon on rich mistresses,
Romantic too, in clumsy, cloudier ways.

87.

There is an ignition lever on the wheel.
Advance. Retard. It could be also French.
Some did not know what frenching was of course,
But grew up playing games about ignition
While modernism passed its palmy days.
The dreams somehow were limited by boyhood
With no belief in possibility
Outside of the romantic's boyish head.
It would be traitorous to attempt translation
Into the real world: the ocean flyer
Never becoming pilot; the general, soldier;
Explorer, traveller; even the great lover
Being slow to learn the rudiments of love.
But still the advance guard held exposed positions.

88.

Girls achieved total being all at once,
Pressing on air like buds or bowls of fruit,
Curved entities which cup what they contain,
Not angular and pointed like the male;
Were intimate with air as blossoms are,
Disturbed, at rest, or crowding here and there
In sudden multitudinous response
To some invisible command or current,
Yet in still self-containment melon-like
Secreting sweetness, one with their own substance.
To be touched. Not to be. Like all perfection,
Reproach, remembrance of another state.
Seeming like dream things, yet more real than he,
The opposite. The other. Yet quintessence.

89.

The blonde chicks in the movies knew the answers,
Moved their behinds ironically, chewed
Gum as the fellow talked, to his discomfort.
With cardboard shoes, two pairs of knickers and
Oddly enough not much that she could sell
In little old New York in twenty-nine
A girl had to watch her chances all the time.
Alone in the big city where the lights
Threw lurid messages of profit on
The bedroom wall, they learned the truth, but fast.
You gotta make a buck. You're on your own now.
I'm sorry baby, but it ain't for free.
Some affectations of sophistication.
Steam heat the air of freedom. Leaking shoes.

90.

Romantic Ireland dead as the man said,
If ever it was otherwise, its fated
Mother-loving heroes mouthing clichés
Before a yawn, a dirty joke, a scuffle,
Their lives, their martyrdom's, moved Brother Welsh
To brave deeds with the leather every day,
Their purity, their shining well-scrubbed thoughts.
Made them remote as Íosagán or Patrick,
No real possibilities destroyed
Since death all they asked for, the rope's jerk
Giving a first erection as a last.
We did not even see them as romantic,
The life they wanted grey as the grey schoolyard,
With grey beyond, grey houses and grey clouds.

91.

'The Biggest Show On Earth, A Warner Brothers
Vitaphone Production, Gold Diggers
Of Nineteen Thirty Eight', the net effect
Of those new stockings, forested in rows
Debated and deplored, a blow to morals.
Whether we were, as Father Fahy said,
Small victims of a Jewish plot to make
Satan triumphant, showing us such leg,
Or beneficiaries beyond old dreams,
A trick of light rays and of celluloid
Bringing that shine to eyes of village lads
Who ever thought an eye would get that far
Whatever hands might travel in the dark,
Each kick a blow to something, if not morals.

92.

Let the city open tonight, an unfolding flower
Not yet full blown, glass petals tipped with promise,
Let it greet its lovers with wide embracing tracks,
Narrowing nearer to the nervous centre.
Let the neon signs throw roses on shining pavements
As the dusk of summer softens each separate vista.
Let the tigerish hide of the quarter proclaim a fierce
Energy in this decadence, this danger.
Let all be famous, but everyone too be anonymous,
Let all find their old friends, but stalk expectant
Through swathes of faces, seeking the lovely stranger.
Let the wicked streets be happy, the happy ones wicked,
Let us tremble, so great the depravity, lurid the darkness,
But come to the leafy gardens, finding the loved one.

93.

Let the city be spectacle, circus, arena this evening,
Its justification sensation, its poetry wonder,
And let it cling fast to its colours, unholy and gaudy
Forgetting the facts of its life, its grimness of purpose.
Let the news that is flashing through bulbs on facades be exciting
But innocent also. Let crowds in another city
Bring down a dictator, lone ocean flyers be sighted,
Sporting events bring riches to all the participants,
Records be broken in every sort of endeavour,
The roar of the crowd sustain the elation of sacrifice.
But over it all, like the neon red glow on the clouds,
The sense of a future the artists have comprehended
Demanded in manifestoes, foreshadowed in dramas,
Simple, electric and complex, achieved like the morning.

94.

This is a mother, not a fatherland,
It nags its children, asking endless love,
Is helpless as a mother to provide,
And, sheltering them from the rough world beyond
Its curtains it unfits them for the streets,
Where others are home. Her weapons are
Reproach, reminders of their lineage,
Their difference, the wrongs that have been done
To her and them, above all of the pain
That life has cost her and the sacrifice
She daily makes to fit them to undo
Such wrongs at last. No wonder that her children
Absorb it all as one confused long lesson.
She suffers for the sin of giving birth.

95.

We went to Brighton in our Little Nine,
The open touring model Leslie bought
On what was called H.P. A gorgeous day,
The sky was somehow deep, you know, like heaven,
I thought the bubbling tar might melt the tyres
And Leslie laughed, called me a silly juggins.
He was a lovely driver, doing forty
Once we were free of Staines. Its tommy rot
To tell us now that people weren't happy.
We had our own nice house, a tudor villa,
Which was the new thing then, a vacuum cleaner,
Dance music on the wireless, lovely murders.
Of course the war was still to come, that Hitler,
But it all seemed somehow new then, somehow modern.

96.

The trouble was that Busby Berkeley's girls,
Feet aching slinging hash or after twenty
Takes of the subway scene makes little difference,
Conflicted with a fiction still wrapped up
And packaged like the romaunts of the roses
Once read in old Provence. A modest female
Who yielded only to a courtly male
And never showed a flesh-curve to a stranger.
Freud said you pitch it high and then it's low.
Debasement part of it, dichotomies,
Something born not of bodies but of minds
Returning there. Oh sure I gave him head.
She didn't know, though, what went on in his.

97.

And we have sat, intent, in scuffed red plush
In scented darkness, watching Gable go
While someone else stayed home, back at the ranch
Perhaps, or at the base, neat, zipped or starched,
But hot for his returning underneath.
So many ages lasted the male dream,
Coming to us in tattered form while war
Ripped skies apart and Papa Hem rejoiced.
The scripts all said the girls were sweet on Clark,
But whether for his martial prowess or
His moustache…? Know the heart of maid
We may not, but the heart of man we know,
Mankind that is, both sexes interlocked
In senile dreams and conflicts, both as one.

III

98.

Everyone believed the Commandant
Lived such a wonderful life. I had my cosy,
Clean well-tended quarters where I could
Retire and be at peace with wife and children.
Her garden was a paradise of flowers.
The children could roam free, their every wish
Attended to. The prisoners who worked
In house and garden never tired of doing
Small kindnesses for both my wife and children.
What people did not know was how I worried
How when at night I stood beside the transports
Or at the crematorium or fire-pits
I thought at length about my family,
Fearing for them in the uncertain future.

99.

And then there was my work. My sense of duty
Has always made life much more difficult
For me than for my colleagues. I worked hard,
Perhaps too hard, at everything I did,
And when they offered me another post
Which meant promotion and which I accepted,
I was at first unhappy. My involvement
With all I did at Auschwitz was so great
That I could not at first detach myself.
What I regret most now though is that this
Exaggerated conscientiousness
Deprived me of more time I could have spent
With my dear wife and children and intruded
On happy evenings spent with them at home.

100.

In the foyer of the Royal Festival Hall,
Great sarcophagus of the forties hope
That wars are fought for art-styles, liberation,
The English in community at last,
The soldiers of the avant garde at home,
An uptight crowd sips its pre-ordered drinks.
Here and there sounds the proper loud haw haw
But most have accents pining on a leash,
Dying a lifetime death in snuffles, whines.
They come in business suits or smart black dresses,
Dating each other after work or sharing
An anniversary with someone's parents.
It is the interval. The chords will wake,
True and transcendent. Then they'll all go home.

101.

A low black storm cloud stains the sky towards Southwark,
The water darkens, pocks and seems to thicken.
The concrete of the Hayward Gallery
Darkens as well. Stains gain an inch or two.
The modern ages as it surely must.
The railway age still lives. It clanks and drags
Another lease of life from Charing Cross
Over the river into Waterloo,
But *modernismus* did not change the world.
And art alas does not explode our lives.
These blocks being what they seem encapsulate
Its shock and seal it off. Like large transformers
They feed out to suburbia a current
Sufficient for an ordered people's needs.

102.

A path was laid to the door of the officers' quarters
Of cinders cleared from the incinerators.
Why did they order this? Why wish to walk
On such black ash so often, be reminded
(Which no one wants) of the job in their spare time?
It was not ideal material.
Ashes would cling to highly polished boots
And in wet weather need some scraping off.
Was it a symbol of their victory,
So that each exit and return was dancing?
Was it of humorous intent, a laddish joke?
Or was it merely an indifference,
Abysmal, mortal, deep within their being
And lurking in the arteries of our world?

103.

Though Reich had said the real one must come first,
One day we had a sexual revolution.
Newspapers dangled girls like carrot bunches
Before male wage slaves on their way to work.
While real girls with minis to their eyebrows
Still had mysterious babies to look after
And solipsists abounded in the bars,
Technology brought Tahiti to the suburbs.
In Switzerland gnomes counted pills and profits
And dropped Repression as a ruling principle,
Installing Emulation there instead.
This was accounted freedom. Many said a decadence.
The flower children thought it was the dawn.
Perhaps the truth lay somewhere in between.

104.

The strip clubs did a roaring trade, well not
Exactly roaring, more a gasp for breath.
The pleasure the packed patrons knew when those
Red curtains rose and all strained glumly forward
Was not so much the happy product of
Permissiveness as early prudery,
Sweet culture shock sustained by inhibition,
For some depending on a thin illusion:
The girls were modest as the next door neighbour
Suffering shame at such extreme exposure.
Skin's palled a bit since then. There's too much of it
And 'showing pink' is the thing in such resorts.
For the time being. Coals to Newcastle.
Diminishing returns an iron law.

105.

Sweet culture shock, sustained throughout our time
In never-ending variations on
That simple theme established long ago.
The modest maidens, manly boys abashed
By their own boldness on a forest path
Have something left to shed, but when it's gone,
The geese which were so rich, the scaly dragons
Considerately following at heel,
To prove the boys all men, the demons who
Ate crumbs from such high tables thankfully,
Will they be then succeeded by the devils
Of accidia and emptiness, chimeras
Prowling the concrete roadways of the suburbs
As far removed from instinct as from joy?

106.

For many then sweet shock was part of summer.
Her going down was really going down
Into breath-stopping depths, the sonar sounder
Ticking the heartbeats off. Hair trailing back
Soft, heavy as she went, she dived far, far
Beneath her sisters in their Sunday best.
Dear Father Baudelaire, you said that sex
Was nothing much without the sense of sin.
Without abandon, sense of desecration,
Freud said, debasement, which may be a sin.
O sinking girl, please don't do down too far.
Put on your skirt and blouse again on heights
From which the depths of such falls can be measured
And let us still feel that sweet shame for you.

107.

Who watch the children anxiously lest they
Through mere familiarity with flesh
And flesh curve, bronzed all over now,
Return to paradise, see eye to eye,
The blue to blue, the grey to grey or green,
Not knowing old concealments and kept straight
By early love flow; hypocrite, you think
The streets too much resemble that lost garden,
Tight denims everywhere and nipples showing.
Don't worry. There'll be barriers enough
Whatever about yours. In this permissive
Age I've seen them huddle by the gables
Of the two bedroom houses in Ringsend,
Wrapped in each other, cloth and winter wind.

108.

Besides, the two beside the river bank
Were parentless, the Doctor was not there
To wag his finger, speak of introjection,
'Parental prohibitions and commands…
Behaviour patterns, good or ill, becoming
Without our conscious credence, observation
The voice of our own super ego, warning
Prohibiting, suppressing…' And so forth.
Yes, it could take a long and weary time
Before we'd all be fit for a new Eden,
The neuroses of the mothers visited
On daughters, who in turn would pass them on.
In fact he's almost saying, sins of fathers,
Right back to Adam's, the original.

109.

Ms Carter is good on class and on the fact
That privilege extends to sex as well,
Not just in terms of what is sold out straight,
Women or ceiling mirrors, water beds,
Hugh Hefner's forms of happiness or forms
Of cosmic fear, but also what you do
When the landlord's on the premises, at the door,
Both parties' nerves all shot with work or worry,
You are living with your in-laws, on the sofa,
Or when the walls are thin, the kids awake.
And then there is what your culture thinks is proper,
Keeping the light on even, travelling,
Over those lovely undulances, making
An evening of love's by-ways, making friends.

110.

If once it was the union of two souls
Meeting like storm-blown altitudinous ghosts,
A meeting which, however passionate,
Whatever that word meant on such bleak heights,
Was a bit cloudy, in our time it's been
Two bodies plus two psyches fusing somehow,
Or two mute bodies, urgent, ardent, thoughtless,
Or even one psyche, fondling its obsessions,
Which were the question and the answer too:
The challenge which contained the secret password,
The dread place which, when entered, could be heaven,
The pain which could burn into ecstasy,
The interrogation which could free us from
The torture and might speak our truth at last.

111.

Although conservatives will argue it–
There are flat-earthers also, travelled men
Who have been around the world and still have doubts –
Will even claim from their experience
That the conjunction we all hoped for, that
Of course we've all had faked for us by times,
Is a quite real phenomenon and common
The evidence suggests it's like the Yeti.
Take comfort if you must from text-book stories
Of joys made possible by 'grind of bone
On pubic bone' or 'tug on lips of vulva'
That union is gone, what we might even call
The common or garden one, except in movies.
The question is, why was it so important?

112.

As in old Lawrence's once notorious book,
Vide pages one eight one and one eight two
Of the prosecuted Penguin, the bit which
Caused all the fuss in fateful nineteen sixty.
Describing how his heroine responded
Old Redbeard almost writes in iambics, such as
'A strange slow thrust of peace, far down inside her...'
'And ever, at the quick of her, the depths...'
'And closer plunged the palpable unknown
Till suddenly the quick of all her plasm...'
'She knew herself,' he tells us, 'touched, the con-
summation was upon her. She was gone'.
There are five 'deepers'. Depth charge stuff all right.
The swinging sixties came in with a bang.

113.

And prosecuting counsel asked the jury
If they would like their daughters, wives or servants
To read it if they left it lying round.
In nineteen sixty, year of great departures.
He should have said their wives or gamekeepers.
Perhaps we have progressed a little since
And also since he wrote about those women.
'That are the devil to bring off at all.'
'The sort that's dead inside; but dead; and know it.'
That won't come when you come 'and bring themselves off',
Its pretty clear how when he speaks of 'writhing'.
And then the diatribe on lesbians.
'They're nearly all', he says. And he could kill them.
The obscenity was not what it was charged with.

114.

Well, lets be charitable, old D.H.
Was blundered around in '28,
A pioneer and maybe too misled
By Frieda, for whatever selfless motive.
But what about the chaps who've written since,
The chaps, we won't say chauvinists, renowned
As much for their adventures as their art.
In their hip books the obliging girls beneath
Our hero twist like salmon in a weir
And ask for nothing but the mighty poke.
And since it's only recently they've written
Of other forms of consummation what
We're up against is a really stunning question:
What happens to the half of modern fiction?

115.

They used to tell us one should go to war
To get to know some things and meet some people.
You form a false view from your ivory tower.
And there was once a school of novelists
Who said they had outfaced the snotty bull.
Been barkeeps, shipped as ordinary seamen,
Shot lions in brown Africa, backed winners,
Sleeping with many women as they went.
All this in aid of knowing things about
The argot, the emotions and the facts
And proving they were men, not just mere writers.
Strange that the lads with legends trailing tall
Should know so very little about sex.
Their beddings egotistic, like their wars.

116.

There was supposed to be a Stella Gardens sequence
To put Yeats and his tower in their place
For, after all, a visitor I had
Opined our little quarter had been built
For the aristocracy of labour – dockers,
Violent and bitter men perhaps when drinking.
The master bedroom measured twelve by six,
The other, square but smaller had no window
Since someone built the kitchen up against it.
The loo was out of doors. I don't complain.
In fact the Stella poems, like extensions
Projected, never started for the want
Of money, time and energy, were meant
To celebrate, as he did, rootedness.

117.

Or anyway a roofing. 51
Stella Gardens, Dublin, was the first
House that I ever owned, almost the first
Object of any kind except for books
And once, a car, although I was a bit
Past what old Dante called the middle of
The path which is our life. Am past it still.
So here I settled down in seventy-two
With wife and children. Iseult seventeen
And Sarah almost eight. I managed two
And sometimes up to four effusions weekly
Facing the bedroom wall, my paper strewn
Behind me on the bed. There were no stairs
Or battlements to pace upon in Stella.

118.

And yet I was embattled in the way
That most of those who are embattled are
In our society. I feared the post,
The admonition from the EBS
Which threatened to uproot me every month,
The ESB which threatened instant darkness,
The GPO which threatened severance.
Yeats said, describing some half mounted gent,
'A man so harried that he seemed to be
Not one, but all mankind's epitome.'
Well even a free-lance's situation
Though scarcely known to sociologists
Can still be seen in terms of common struggle.
Or so at least I, right or wrong, determined.

119.

I joined the NUJ. I wrote long pieces
About the need of state support for artists,
Tried to define an order in which art
Might find itself the breath of common being.
Some well-known ghosts appeared reproachful
'That's phony, all that politics and stuff.'
It wasn't, but I felt a traitor to
The long tradition of the man alone,
Deriding all sides, driven out by all,
To feast on his own heart in scorn and joy,
The central one, in Europe anyway
Since Baudelaire surveyed the damned in Paris,
And one which part of me would still respond to,
As to no other myth of sanctity.

120

The docks were dying. In Stella some had taken
Three thousand quid redundancy, grim word
Grim prospect too, although they didn't know that.
They'd sling a hook no more, but stay in bed,
Drink pints and read the paper, have a bob
On something that Our Traveller Correspondent
Thought might oblige.(Of course it mostly didn't.)
Technology had freed them, so they thought,
The new container dock just down the river
Where ten unloaded tonnage that a hundred
Had fought to handle in the bad old days.
In fact inflation, poised to take off, took.
They were wiped out, their little lump made useless,
And left without work, money, peace of mind.

121.

Their hope was not in heavy hours down holds
Where flour dust choked you or on docksides where
The east wind up the river scorched the cable.
Their hope was pleasant idleness, not work.
A decent option if you'd worked and could
Feel that you'd done your bit and made provision,
Furnished the parlour, built a bathroom on,
Brought kids up who would not disgrace their mother.
It's not of course 'authentic living' (to
Quote Heidegger) nor would it do for me
Who wanted idleness but work as well
Which gave life meaning, was its sweetest solace.
At least our interests did not conflict.
All I would do was add what they wanted.

122.

I brought O'Flaherty to Fitzharris's,
An old *condottier,* he said, a killer.
He sat there, head a carved-out block, and talked
Unreconstructed rubbish by the yard:
The second Dempsey-Tunney fight, the time
That Michael Collins had some fellow shot.
They didn't know who he was, but later on
He passed a little into local legend,
The man who had done great things, some said for Ireland.
'I did it my way' passing Beggar's Bush.
It was not true of them, perhaps of him.
He'd had some sort of stab at it all the same,
As everyone should have, even workers, husbands.

123.

No wide-eyed women loving martial ardour,
The striped ski-slopes precluding the sublime,
Not even causes left or marching columns,
The bomb, the last machine, no myth of godship,
The gas works an industrial exhibit.
A time of lost poetic, me and you,
Red Mars, the moonshots, Marilyn Monroe.
So many poets unhappy in this time,
Sucking the childhood tap root, lovely life-juice,
Milk churns or tweed-capped fathers at the mill,
Searching for fathers even further back,
In the long past, last storehouse of poetic,
The dolmen on the bare front of the hill,
The prehistoric haze, the low sun burning.

124.

Although no pastoral is possible:
No one can really say the dolts can teach us
To mend our ways or give obedience grace,
To be more faithful to the wives they fumbled
Or stiffen ourselves against the east wind cutting
Clichés to ribbons, crunching graveside gravel:
Out of the genes we still make something, though
We are alone here with the jets in fenland,
Grey sea receding towards the infinite,
An ancestor is much, a tribe is better:
We call on Anglo-Saxon, Celt, and Dane,
Whoever dug the ditch or hewed the roofbeams,
To give us somehow oneness with our wasteland,
Though not of course the sort their devils gave.

125.

At Robert Kennedy's funeral the female
Mourners wore mini skirts to the mid thigh.
They were in black of course, clothes *haute couture*,
And skirts were short in 1968.
Their lovely legs and sad expressions made
A deep impression on the viewers in
The Sunset Bar in Des Moines, Iowa.
We watched them travel up the escalators
As they arrived at Pennsylvania Station
And felt another surge of sympathy
As the long limo drew up at the steps
And Jackie carefully got out at last.
It isn't easy to get in or out
Of autos wearing skirts of extreme shortness.

126.

Elvis the liberated liberator
When he was liberated into fame
Gave nightly parties to attract the girls,
Who came in droves. He liked them young
And as innocent-seeming as was plausible.
Those who had been before knew that the King
Would take his pick towards 2 a.m. or so,
When a specially lucky few were asked upstairs,
Told laughingly to strip down to their panties
(He had a preference for virgin white)
And wrestle with each other while he watched.
If afterwards they went to bed with him
They kept their panties on, those small white shields,
Though stained with semen shielding him from something.

127.

As a child, he said, he had seen two little girls
Tussling in some backyard, their knickers showing.
His liberation was a narrowing vista,
A moment and a gleam. He made home movies
Of hired girls, fighting, watched them on his own.
But, to be fair, he liked girls' company
And had his steadies even that he romped with
In almost film-script fashion: boy meets girl,
The music's new, it's still the same old dream
And love is still an all-American game.
He could not bear to watch the films he starred in
But had romantic yearnings all the same
And knew some sort of love and married twice.
Millions have longings they can never share.

128.

If he hadn't been liberated he'd have probably
Passed for quite normal, would in other times,
And must have tried to be with his two wives.
Far gone in drugs as he was and then also
Fixated on imagination's fix,
The chances are it wasn't a success.
The sixties have a lot to answer for.
The movies shocked his Memphis bully boys
When they discovered them, or so they said.
Their first arousings must have been much simpler
And Memphis does not know that every oddball
Is but an infant, doomed to a response.
The complex in a life would be beyond it,
Its decadences heavy macho stuff.

129.

That delicate first comer shall be king
Doubtless, the gazing infant never safe
From visions of thighs or stocking tops or bra straps,
The god descending on a beach, in boudoirs,
In the school playground or a circus tent,
In baths, the dentist's, sweet induction comes
Anyhow, anywhere, through any chance,
A cousin's shoulders in an aertex vest,
A blue-clad junction underneath a gym slip,
A bared knee genuflecting in the chapel,
Praise be he shoots his arrows everywhere,
In mother's bedroom, bless his little heart,
While the drums roll, the chorus wheels, or while
The home side snatches victory at hockey.

130.

And blessed are those to whom he brings obsessions
Accounted normal, manageable, sweet,
Unbiddable as honeysuckle scent,
But accepted in the joyous jumble sale
Where slips, straps, smalls and circumstance compose
A flood, a breaking foam in which to drown
And bare arms, insteps, breasts and backs assemble
A hierarchical heaven singing praise.
Less lucky those whose first stab is bizarre,
Like Rousseau when his lovely guardian beat him,
And doomed the doleful ones whose apparition
Comes tinged with agonies of other sorts,
Hatred of mother metamorphosed to love
Of scrambling girls, bared, hot, humiliated.

131.

O lady of the moon whose profiled face
Halts our walk homeward underneath the trees,
Shine on unblessedness your blessing now,
Wed our desire with our desire to please.
Lonely Actaeon saw your bared, pale flesh
Through celluloid of water, silver bright,
And stood prolonging this unholy joy
Feasting on nerve ends in the moon's limelight.
You turned your back, autogamous as he,
But knew him gazing still on that expanse,
Turning to stasis what should be a dance.
Turning to wrong and sulkiness what should
Have touched with joy that whole nocturnal wood.

132.

So you reversed the roles, you would hunt too
And not for satisfaction of the flesh
But rage of justice which you would endure
When in the thicket you would see him thrash,
Torn by those dogs, the fiercest time had reared,
Perfected in dissection of their game,
Actaeon suffered doubly, dog rends, mauls,
And also incremental wounds of shame.
But if you through the agency of dogs
Gained rapture of revenge and righteous pangs,
You learned that also near a nearer bone
There would be severings by the self-same fangs.
So now let hunters and their prey be one,
Be pray, be hunter and all preying done.

133.

And *qua tu fait de ta jeunesse*, my lad?
I sold a lot of it to a pension fund.
We all sell, every one of us, to buy.
It wasn't bad, the routine of the office,
The country girls across the corridor,
The weak-end booze-up, sometimes a good bang.
He sells his brain-time, buys a new Toyota,
A house on mortgage and the company
Of bright-eyed children, a neurotic wife.
He sells some brawn-time for a feel of breasts,
The pints and fags, the outings with the lads.
She sells some handling, an insertion or
A reluctant suck without the rubber for
The well-being of the child that bastard left her.

134.

Dowson found harlots cheaper than hotels.
He might not now, they pay high rents as well.
And neither would he find appeasement knowing
The dear-bought freedoms of bohemia
Denied to the respectable: strange term
From days when Ormsby, Gore and Atkinson
Knew that in order to be duns, not debtors,
They had to keep the straight and narrow or
Go sneaking out at night like Jack the Ripper.
Nowadays money and a mohair suit
Confer more freedoms on them than he'd have.
Now while he'd pine they're sucked off every night
And much respected for it by their peers
Who can afford hotel and harlot too.

135.

And where the system functions as I should,
The competition being keen and sharp,
If Dowson had a buck or two at all,
Having knuckled down a bit, say one semester,
A novel, culture noddings on the telly,
Sometimes at least he'd find he could afford
The lesser forms of harlotry, though lesser
In fact so far out by our fathers' standards,
Or even by Symons's somewhat garish lights,
That dealings in the eschatology, the end
Of lives, or just of eras, plus debasement
As he did, he might come to wonder were
The harlots who were offerings such delights
As eager for an ending as himself.

136.

If that famous curious visitor
From lifeless mars were still to come to earth
He would report (although, agreed, he couldn't)
That the inhabitants of this crawling place
Were all obsessed by something they called 'love'.
This was a state of mind, he would conclude,
Whose consequences for the sufferer were
That happiness was now impossible
For him or her without the company
And constant sexual congress with the loved one.
Oddly they used the same word to describe
A feeling many thought it was their duty
To have towards others, family, friends, or even
Their fellow humans, in the lump, at large;

137.

They like to hear, he'd say, fine songs about love.
You hear theses songs at all hours issuing from
Their little radios everywhere you go.
In restaurants, bars, the laundromat, the brothel.
It seems to be the first kind that is sung of.
The wanting to be with and fuck another.
The second as I say is more of a duty,
Grimly and sometimes sadly undertaken.
What's certain is that this strange love emotion
Forlorn, despairing though it sometimes may be.
It's all that's left to them of the sublime
And almost all that's left of their vast searching
For meaning or significance in their state.

138.

After the phone call which the chairman made
To his lordship, still abroad, the towers descended,
Sliced neatly at the base, becoming clouds.
The tramlines stretched unburnished in the sun
And father stayed at home to watch the telly,
Which could not fill the silence with its voices.
His skills an entail, now of no more use.
England which they had gouged and torn and shafted
Rested from agony. Their poets had said
England was parkland, pitheads an offence.
Let it be parkland then, be pastoral,
Dollars and Deutschmarks grass their white-fenced paddocks,
Red steel-flakes rust like leaves into the rivers,
Great oaks return and Arden be again.

139.

The discovery was they did not need the mills,
Satanic, dark or otherwise. The mills,
If mills they were, could be in places
Where yellow men and women without unions
Worked happily in denims day and night
While dividends flowed in to keep the fenced-off
Acres as acres should be kept. The puzzle,
The only one remaining now, was people,
The football-loving people of the cities
Whose differences were bus routes on a map,
The Pennine clefts, the cobbled valleys, endless
Brick yellow streets, who had once been torn like turnips
Out of the clodded fields, their screams unheard
And strangely had some call on England still.

140.

The line might well be drawn through Shakespeare country.
North of the woods of Warwick once had grown
The webs of brick and girder, the black pall
Beneath which a fair-minded people dreamed
Of self-help, co-operation, brotherhood,
While in the grimy mansions perched on hills
The pith was put in maxims: thou gets nowt
For nowt and little enough for tuppence hereabouts.
South of the line was lackey country where
Dickens's clerks had their descendants in
Computer people, form-fillers and chaps
Whose heaven still was hierarchical.
Well, some barbed wire and dogs and stiff policing
Would see the real England still prevail.

141.

On either side of the river laps at smooth
And sterile surfaces, no wharves or pier stakes
Interrupt its fast sequestered flow.
A veil of moving traffic separates
It's dark expanse from Fleet Street and the Strand;
The artery is now where, rubber black,
The safe road takes the many home tonight,
Each Sunday traveller or family
Encapsulated from the world outside.
As dusk falls and the headlights show the rain
The scene seems curiously empty, silent too,
Although the traffic's while is ceaseless and
Car radios interpolate the cries
Of love with bulletins of war and crime.

142.

On the Embankment side the Thames police
Still have a station, though their tin-roofed shed
Seems permanently empty, locked and shuttered.
Corpses, it seems, are rare. Most throw themselves
In front of Tube trains now. In Dickens's time
Watermen trafficked in each tide's sad freight,
Along the Strand an elbowing gaslit crowd
Knew the cold water's nearness, sensed its threat,
And east of here, where homes were haunts and dens,
The middle class imagined mystery
And violence to be modes of life for millions.
Out terrors are both less and more immediate
Than when, quick, fecund, crowded, strangely homelike
The river sucked much closer to the heart.

143.

Sweating Bacardi over a tanned wanton
Who didn't want such baths, his lordship worried
About the electric fence, which didn't seem to
React to niggers somehow. As for dogs,
Those Dobermans were if anything more friendly
To stinking bucks than whites. Could they distinguish?
In fact, now that he came to think of it,
The only thing round here that had strong feelings
About colour was this whore beneath his belly,
Who arched and purred and eyed them at prick level.
He thought of England, green and cool and safe,
Of gravelled drives where no black maniacs walked,
Of servants bred from servants, then of dole queues
Composed of blacks and slackers. Such great problems.

144.

Off boulevards which flame in blue and red,
Like brimstone, where the serried coaches come,
Holiday-coloured, orange, pink and yellow,
Discharging senior citizens to enjoy
At a place Lautrec and La Goulue when eager
Had made a legend in another time,
Some hours of sanitised and distant strip,
Down darker streets are found by the more daring
Privileges which were once a great lord's prize,
The faces cold or pert, some beautiful
And not much marked by this impersonal traffic,
Many which, given other circumstance
To gaze on the high cheek and hollow eyes
Might haunt a true romantic all his days.

145.

The wheat grew thick beside the Roman way,
The curved stalks single, thick impasto strokes.
American grain killed off the market for it,
As, in the eighties, Engels said it would
So now it's pear trees, chemically boosted.
But you still see on the road to the Camargue,
Those yellow cornfields under that blue sky.
He went there in October, so did we.
They were burning stubble, making strips of black,
The flame first poppies, then the short stalks gone.
He never found the calm love of creation
For its own blessed sake, even in this south.
Under those burning suns, intensity
As much his theme as high recessive blue.

146.

In Saintes Marie the Super Etendards
Banged through the sonic barrier, themselves
Almost invisible, tipped vapour trails.
He thought the peasant girls here beautiful
And painted boats, hauled up on the beach shingle.
There are no boats or peasant girls today
Except for pleasure craft, perhaps the blonde
Who pulled beer for the German and his dog.
Its bars and bungalows, apartment blocks
Around a tatty beach. October weather
Like a great shimmering gong, sea dirty bronze.
It's not much as a place of pilgrimage.
The Germans don't come here because of him.
The mutable, the modern now triumphant.

147.

And Arthur Scargill in his madness said,
'I see Jehovah in the wintry sun
Which looks to her like any golden guinea.
I see the lamb of God in England's fields.'
And so on a bright day in England's winter
When Trafalgar Square lies dry and sharp and shadowed
We ask the right to work, close punk rock ranks
Beneath the heavy portico behind
Which shelter many splendid works of art
And underneath Lord Nelson who broke rules
But saved the bacon of the ruling class.
More moral than our rulers we reject
A life of idleness, a lack of aim,
Of purpose, effort, patriotic zeal.

148.

The right to work. Assorted publicists
And politicians who, quite rightly too,
Have no desire to work at any task
Other than those for which they feel they have
An unmistakable vocation, ask
On our behalf the right to other work
And so they might, for its been bred into
The bent and grimy bone, this need to work.
It may be it will cure itself in time,
It may be we will learn to laugh and laze
Our limbs stretched in the sun like animals,
To hunger, sleep and feed and know not it.
Meanwhile we see the dark satanic mills
Recede like visions of Jerusalem.

149.

Max Eastman wrote of meeting them on trains
When under Lenin's leadership the country
Was just emerging from the Civil War.
Middle-aged men with philosophic foreheads,
Motherly, grey-haired women with calm eyes,
A younger woman, sensuous, beautiful.
Who bore herself as if she had once walked
Up to a cannon's mouth. You would enquire,
He said, and you would find these were the veterans,
Taught in infancy to love mankind,
Master themselves, be free from sentiment,
The high traditions of the terrorist movement.
They had learned in youth a new mode from the party,
To think in practical terms, was how he put it.

150.

At a party conference in Moscow Province
A vote of thanks to Stalin was proposed.
Everyone stood and, smiling, clapped and cheered
Quite normally. But this time no one stopped.
No one would risk the dreaded accusation
That they were less admiring than their neighbour,
So it went on and on, a marathon
Display of stamina until at length
Some of the veterans collapsed, exhausted.
These were the veterans Eastman had described
A few short years before, a noble order.
Vowed like a knightly band to heroism
But with their patents of nobility
Not in the past, but in our human future.

151.

Our human future was to be quite other
Than that they had imagined in those years,
Waiting at tram stops in the freezing snow,
Keeping their assignations in the café
With newcomers who brought news from Russia,
Living in libraries under shaded lights.
We know their future now (we know ours too);
Red stars unblinking, sleepless, enigmatic.
Red sun which rose each morning over Moscow;
All seeing, like the God they had forgotten,
All knowing in whose radiance their courage
Melted like dirty, wet, bedraggled snow,
Human reduction to the dirt on which
Historic boot-heels hastened history's end.

152.

Childe Roland to the dark tower came and climbed
The massive steps in natural trepidation.
But when the blonde beyond the blinding fountain
Asked him his name and business, his composure
Returned. He coolly showed his new ID
And obeying bored directions took the bronze
Lift to the fourteenth floor as he'd been told.
He smiled quite naturally at them while he noted
That Evil preferred its girls gaunt, doe-eyed, starving,
And thought it would be nice to get to know
The ones he met, while being quite aware
The person they responded to could never
Be himself. In the Dark Tower all tried
To be as was expected, not themselves.

153.

So he must change, invent and synthesise,
Suppress both cynic and idealist,
And hide as well the hate and tenderness.
He could use some of what he was, with skill
Deploying only aspects of self.
Quite possibly the anarchist, the dreamer,
Used strictly for effect, with guarded tongue,
Might easily impress, beguile or charm,
As had the 'characters' in his former life.
But, after all, what is the self? The much
Discussed, mulled over, moralised about,
True self, was even perhaps mythical,
Was, anyway, a burden from the past.

154.

The first surprise was their delight in order,
Clipping and filing, typing, entering,
As if great things depended on exactness
In every single action. The new world
The Dark Tower was creating was destructive,
Oblivious, wasteful, with no end in view
Save further barren prodigality.
Within was category, calm and care,
The men in agonies of detail, logic,
Foresaw eventualities of every sort;
The slender fingers of half-starved girls
Worked on with cool precision, almost gentle.
The end, in short, was stark and utter madness.
But the means used considerate and sane.

155.

And then one day his work was noticed, he
Was taken down the corridor and through
A padded door, to lunch with Evil in
An inner sanctum. And of course he loved it.
The subtle ambience of power obeyed
In silent smoothness and complicity
Is almost an aesthetic satisfaction.
But also there was something which to most
Of those he knew outside the building's precincts
Would come as a surprise. These men did not
Exude ambition, lust for aggrandisement
Like millionaires – or gangsters – in old movies.
Their gravity, their calm, their humour even,
Spoke only of the burdens that they bore.

156.

How many marches on Trafalgar Square
Since John Burns and Ben Tillett strode with beards
Nailed to their chins and Yeats's young friend stood guard
On documents which could hang William Morris?
The pigeons yield it up again. They know
The scrape and rattle of applause in tannoys
Like pebbles being sucked beneath a wave,
Is not for ever. Tourists will return
Red buses and an active boredom reign.
If Neil Kinnock should go mad and maybe
Pull down the pillars of the gallery,
Proclaim the revolution, would we follow?
Another march ends now. The fringes drift
With furled up banners towards the nearest Watneys.

157.

And bloody right as that American
Said, 'Its no job for white men going down
A mineshaft in a cage and digging coal
While the brief sun shines on a winter morn
And your lungs gather silicon dioxide,
Not any more, not in this day and age.'
Nor any man, nor ever, since it can
Be done mechanically, even done without,
Or if you could get married on their dole
And bring up kids, keep pigeons, punt a bit,
Race whippets, do those other cliché things
That miners are supposed to do, or better
If days brought lovely purpose, clear and sweet
Extensions of each human faculty.

158.

Nor ever wonder if you were scrim-shanking
While others did the work, were just a scrounger,
Nor wonder either what it was supposed
To be about, this weary sort of life,
Nor sweat sometimes at night for fear that they
Would take away your dole or make it smaller,
Now that you'd lost all clout and couldn't even
Withdraw your labour from them any more.
But these are just day dreams. Their doles are not
Sufficient to keep racing pigeons on,
Have a few pints and punt a bit as well,
Hire video and films, buy tapes and records,
Support the heavy hours of idleness
Support life without purpose or achievement.

159.

When Patrick Kavanagh's mother took him to
The circus which had come to Inniskeen,
They saw among the other acts a man
Lifting enormous weights and staggering
Bow-legged around the ring, his biceps, eyeballs,
Bulging with fearful effort. After that
He lay down on a bed of pointed nails.
Attendants placed a plank across his chest.
Ten bashful local louts were then invited
To stand across it, their combined weight being
About a half a ton. The poet observed
It seemed a hard way for a man to earn
His living; but his mother said it was
Better than working anyway, she thought.

160.

'Bring me my bow of burning gold', they sing,
Linked hand in hand on the Labour Conference platform,
Their faces grey after a week of murdering
Tormenting words through composite resolutions
And phrases chosen for inclusiveness.
'Bring me my arrows of desire'. They look
Like their desires, unacted, nursed
Through nights of envy, bonhomie and booze,
The pristine vision dying among details.
Outside is England on an autumn evening,
Skinheads and space-invaders on the front,
The televisions blueing the bow windows.
'I will not cease from mental strife' acquits
His verses of a mere utopian wish.

161.

And here is where Evil was supposed to rule
He even found a sort of fellow spirit,
Of all the most remarkable, whose gaze,
Contemplative, amused, but not unkind,
Rested on Roland while the new recruit
Outlined a project with fresh eagerness
Or offered findings with due indifference.
The intelligent are always lonely, always
In search of fellows; but intelligence
In enterprise at least is not displayed
In inquisition of the heart or conscience
As in the cafés where the jealous poets,
Debarred from action, enviously dissected
Emotions, motives, purities of purpose.

162.

His new friend spoke of the philosophy
– Or rather lack of it – the Dark Tower brought
To its activities. Alone among
The other power-systems on this planet
It was not tempted into ever seeking
To state or to define its ontogenesis.
Why should it bother? It did not appeal
To the Great Dead or seek a mandate from
The ancestors. It had no philosophic
Purpose that could be named, did not pretend
Or claim its power served any Absolute
Or Moral Order in the Universe.
The Dark Tower knew the philosophic vaccum
In which mankind now lived and welcomed it.

163.

Unlike politicians on the podia
Who talked and tried to act as if they were
Able to adumbrate a common purpose
Transcending circumstance and even time,
Or the archaic power-systems still
Slowly decaying or collapsing round it.
The Tower did its work without pretence
To knowledge of man's ultimate destiny;
But was, he emphasised with almost passion,
The most important agent yet of history.
All others sought to limit and define:
The Tower alone to find and satisfy
Man's existential nature through his needs
And wishes, fantasies, hopes and desires.

164.

And what more noble end could be than this one?
Or what more democratic than response
To every wish, expressed through mechanisms,
Invisible, infallible, unerring,
Machinery so natural that its working
Seemed but a law of nature liberated.
It fought no wars; it summoned to no flags,
Its power did not depend on sad prescription,
On moral exhortation, old deceits.
It used its influence only to ensure
The neutral freedom which was necessary
To let it do its work, entice mankind
To enter on its future, realise
Without hypocrisy its actual nature.

165.

When Roland woke at night now in his new
White decorated, minimalist pad
From which all evidences of a soul
Thrashing around amongst its discontents,
Passing enthusiasms, short-lived fits of purpose,
All the disorder of unordered life
Lived in the hope of love and revelation,
Has been removed, replaced by the quite simple
Serenity of a resolved equation,
He heard above the murmur of the traffic,
Going about his business in the darkness
A voice ask what it profited to save
One's solipsistic, self-regarding soul
If one should lose the real world in that saving?

166.

Now for the first time in his life he was
Able to see the visible result
Of mental effort, speculative thought,
Theory and calculation. Once his joy
Had been fitting thought to loving thought,
Premise to logical conclusion in
An ecstasy of clear contingency,
Now he was like an engineer who sees
The long curved line which was mere concept still,
Become a bridge tectonic, actual,
Hold fast and bear its calculated weight.
The metaphors his world had used for thought –
Foundation, edifice, conclusion even –
Now seemed to him mere childishness, pretence.

167.

The speaker in smart. No doubt at all of that.
His glasses glint. His punch lines are quite punchy,
And smart or not his heart's in the right place,
Which is to say, exactly where ours is.
Then why this vague unease one knows so well?
When the unanimous resolutions start
And everybody bleeds for the good cause
Why is one guilty, with them or against?
I listened at the NUJ, the protests,
Apartheid, Solidarity, the lot.
They applauded, right on cue, with righteous faces,
And laughed, with righteous glee, at easy sallies.
Why does being right seem wrong? I wondered,
Or protest seem so like complacency?

168.

No enemies, not even the milk-drinking
Fifteenth floor ghosts with six-inch fingernails
Who summoned starlets to share death with them,
All ownership at last invisible,
And moral like ourselves. Just like our own
Its grave deferral to the facts and figures
Appearing on innumerable screens,
Unalterable, though we peer again.
It has no separate nature, good or bad.
We share its greeds, its lapses, love of children.
Even its thin benevolence is ours.
Yet it commands earth; sickens crops;
Blights forests; poisons oceans; hangs, a cloud
Of grim foreboding over river valleys.

169.

But gives life too, inspires the dance performed
By almost everyone. Scarcely an action done
But to placate this power, by day and night,
All the great rushing life of cities in its service,
The crowds on the long clicking escalators,
The tangled traffic in the street outside,
The courteous workers, filing, copying,
The managers who speak into recorders.
All listen for its promises, commands,
Little is done without its sly approval,
Little for God, of course, but equally
Little to celebrate our mere existence.
Even when we pause, to dream or to create.
It measures out our moments like a meter.

170.

And philosophic hate the holiest,
Think of the brevity of this our state
The scope and eagerness of the human mind,
The sense of possibility we're born with,
Then of the lives maimed even while the child
Creates its first imagos, even in
The bed of sad conception, wondrous souls
Reduced already to a wretchedness
The animals would pity if they knew.
Most of life dull acceptance of pretence
Drudgeries for no clear end or reason,
For mere perpetuation of our kind,
Commerce, convention, avarice and power
Conspiring to construct the traps we're caught in.

171.

The wants he satisfied with his new-found wealth
Were strangely theoretical, as are the wants
The rest of us are told we have. He bought
What young executives are supposed to buy,
An Audi V8 4.2 whose engine
Was capable of greater speeds than ever
Could be attained on any actual road,
Gadgets which he never had occasion
To use or which were quickly superseded
By different models; cameras, recorders:
Ways to reproduce the images
Of places he had no wish to revisit
And never called to mind, aids which destroy
True evocation, memory, the past.

172.

Of course he had affairs. With gaunt, hard girls
Not inlike those he'd seen on the first day,
But more ambitious, possibly more able.
Nor were they like the girls he'd known before
In many sad cafés. These girls were not
The aimless waifs of that now lost existence.
They shared the Tower's *weltanschauung*, its values,
And though he didn't know that for some time
The Tower's ability to diminish, empty
And etiolate the sense of what was possible.
Even in bed, engaging in the acts
The magazines permitted, which were many,
There was this ebb of possibility,
This strange foreclosure of the human bounds.

173.

'I must do a starry night with cypresses'.
Beside the clothes line where we hung the washing
Out at night to catch the morning sun
The cypress grove grew black against the blue black,
The stars beyond it splintered and enlarged.
(Myopia makes the stars more starry still).
His moral suffering was very great.
Mine too, but his was madness, beyond cause.
In fact one finds it hard to comprehend.
His letters are no help, religious horror
Is not the same as moral self-reproach.
The modern has betrayed us as the mad
Him. We are still found to the moral law,
Nor Vincent nor Gauguin excuses us.

174.

An *asile* is a refuge, the sad name
Suggests the mad have more to fear from us
Than we from them. We saw the patients walk
In shambling line as I had seen them once
In Enniscorthy, County Wexford, walk
The grounds of the asylum by the river.
Terrified, hoping none could climb the wall.
Although I know a little better now
In rational terms at least, I still hung back
Till they had vanished through the studded door
Which opens off the cloister before going
To have a look at Zadkine's sculpture of him.
I wondered what the patients thought of it.
A hero of their kind, and of our world.

175.

The Dark Tower stood, the tallest of the tall.
But strangely light and immaterial,
Its surface chaste, sheer, almost featureless,
A shining object, its reflecting glass
Making it sphinx-like, answering no question.
Acquisitiveness and greed proclaimed at last
As ruling principles of mankind's being,
Without decree, alike without concern
For past or future, or eternity.
The tower decided for humanity,
Whether some ate or starved, what crops they grew,
Whether they lived in tents of sacking by
Streams thick with sewage fringing smoky cities
Or scratched the soil in gangs on mountain slopes.

176.

Roland delighted in its outward beauty,
Its chisel-thin, cloud-piercing, neutral form,
Unmoving against flowing fields of sky,
Now seemed to his Platonic, universal.
And also loved its inward-looking order,
The murmur of its air ducts soothing, steadying
Its calm and rational process of decision.
But it had roots as well, which stretched far under
Continents, seas and cities, reaching, gripping,
Blind, hungry, pale and white-tipped tentacles.
Engorging, pulping as they grew and fattened,
Groping for profit in their sightless searching,
Grasping the crumbling substances around,
Sucking the sweet sustenance from earth.

177.

When he was better and the weather summer
He sat up in the meadow there and painted
The edge of the Alpilles, the hanging sun,
A cornfield in the foreground, hot, bright yellow.
There is a reaper in the field, no symbol,
Not the grim death that he had done before
It's flooded with its light and brims like prayer,
Unlike the twisted olives in the garden,
Done in the cold before his madness lifted.
Though some would like to pray or like their work
To be a prayer or an affirmation,
Lacking his madness, we lack his belief,
The agony of the olives, the corn's bounty,
Both alien to us in our threatened world.

178.

Quite shocking visions of despair and horror
Expend themselves against our approval,
The modulated space of boardrooms, bedrooms.
Are dealt in blandly by sophisticates
Who know the price and the occluding jargon.
Nor are 'our merchant classes' philistines.
By their remote command a clean, lit place
White, windowless, unshadowed, limbo-like
Accommodates an endless series
A passionless acceptance reigns within
These air-conditioned spaces which absorb
To the faint murmur of a distant duct
The last assault waves of the avant garde.

179.

Ask not what end, inquiring traveller,
Is served, what grim need to placate a god
Or worship him, what visions, definitions of
Our destiny, our purpose threw up these
Audacious towers to shine in evening light.
The sun, a crucible of nuclear rage,
Knows nothing of such ends: it thrummed out rays
Of heat until the ooze transformed itself.
Money's convulsions too are life-giving,
Neutral, imply no purpose in our hearts,
But blazed upon this rock to make Manhattan
Rise in resplendence, such a culmination
Of history seen at sunset from the harbour,
Meaningless, astonishing and simple.

The following places and people, sometimes speaking directly, have not been identified in the text.

61. Vienna.

67. Vladimir Lenin.

70-71. Pablo Picasso.

74. Berlin, 2 August 1914. Friedrich Meineke.

77. Ferdinand Léger.

78-81. Vladimir Lenin.

98-99. Rudolf Hess, Commandant of Auschwitz. He is quoted almost verbatim here.

108. Sigmund Freud.

145-146, 173-174, 177. Vincent Van Gogh.